UNDER$PENT

**How I broke my shopping
addiction & buying habit
without dramatically
changing my life**

RACHEL SMITH

First published in 2015 by Rachel Smith
Paperback edition published in 2016 by Rachel Smith

National Library of Australia Cataloguing-in-Publication entry

Creator:	Smith, Rachel, author.
Title:	Underspent : how I broke my shopping addiction & buying habit without dramatically changing my life / Rachel Smith.
ISBN:	9780994563538 (paperback)
Subjects:	Compulsive shopping. Shopping.
Dewey Number:	616.8584

Cover design and book production: Vanessa Battersby
Internal design: Michael Hanrahan Publishing & Vanessa Battersby
Printed in Autralia by McPherson's Printing

CONTENTS

INTRODUCTION

On New Year's Eve 2012, I decided to quit shopping. I pledged and promised to buy nothing new or second-hand for one whole year (2013).

I failed.

I saw buying nothing as a hardship filled with doom and gloom, like a year of punishment. 'Negativity creates negativity'—my year of no buying lasted just four months.

In 2014, I tried again.

Second time around, I saw buying nothing new or second-hand for a year as an exciting opportunity, an adventure and a whole new way to live my life—a lifestyle experiment.

Positive thinking creates positive experiences. I succeeded.

I didn't buy anything new or second-hand for one year.

I quit shopping for 365 days.

It was one of the best years of my life. I saved 38 per cent of my net annual salary and I didn't dramatically change my life to do it.

ABOUT THIS BOOK

THE OUTCOMES FOR ME

For me, the ultimate result of implementing the seven steps I've set out in this book was:

▶ being Underspent—spending less than usual (I was spending less money than was required and expected)

▶ breaking my impulse shopping addiction and habit of buying 'stuff'

▶ saving 38 per cent of my net (take-home) annual salary

▶ being happier and more content.

WHO THE BOOK IS FOR

I've written this book because I want to share how I broke my impulse shopping addiction and habit of buying 'stuff', without dramatically changing my life.

I didn't buy anything for a year. That's extreme.

This book is for men and women who want to quit shopping and save money.

WHAT THE BOOK DOES

In this book, I'll tell you what I did. I won't tell you what to do. I only want to share the tools that worked for me. This is a practical guide for men and women who want to quit shopping and save money.

THE BOOK'S CONTENTS

The book is divided into four parts:

▶ **Part 1: Houston, we have a problem**
   Part 1 explains the problems associated with shopping and buying, as well as the reasons why we shop so much, why we overspend and what triggers our shopping and spending.

▶ **Part 2: My story**

In this section, I share my story and the seven things I love about quitting consumerism.

▶ **Part 3: The sticking points**

This part explains the seven sticking points we face when trying to break addictions and habits, and seven personal barriers we may have to overcome, like boredom and fear of missing out.

▶ **Part 4: The seven-step process**

Part 4 explains the seven-step process that worked for me, including identifying my passions, making a budget, getting people in place to help, using everything that I already had and having fun.

✳

With everything that you've read so far, I know exactly what you're thinking:

> 'Can I really break my impulse shopping addiction and habit of buying "stuff" without dramatically changing my life?'

Yes, you can—and you can do it right now. And in the remainder of this book, I'm going to tell you what I did and share what worked for me.

PART 1:
HOUSTON, WE HAVE
A PROBLEM

SO WHAT IS THE PROBLEM?

'Normal is getting dressed in clothes that you buy for work and driving through traffic in a car that you are still paying for in order to get to the job you need to pay for the clothes and the car, and the house you leave vacant all day so you can afford to live in it.'

Ellen Goodman

The rising cost of living is one of the biggest issues in Australia, America and the UK.

► The average Australian adult spends the first eight weeks of each year working just to pay for their car.

► According to the media, the average American owns 3.5 credit cards and owes US$15,799 in credit card debt.

► Three out of five American families can't pay off their credit card debts.

▶ In the UK, someone is declared insolvent or bankrupt every five minutes, and a property is repossessed every eighteen minutes.

▶ Thirteen per cent of Australian adults and seventeen per cent of Aussie kids live below the poverty line.

▶ The average American spends more than twelve hours each month shopping.

▶ Apparently, there are more shopping malls in America than high schools.

▶ There are more than eighteen million shopaholics in the United States.

▶ Ninety-three per cent of teenage girls in the United States say shopping is their favourite activity.

▶ Australians, as a nation, spend over AU$12 billion a year on more than one billion fashion items.

▶ Five per cent of all waste in Australian landfill is discarded clothing.

▶ The UK's Citizens Advice Bureau deals with more than 7,000 debt problems every day.

▶ Americans spend US$1.2 trillion each year on goods and services they don't absolutely need, including spending US$350 million on pet Halloween costumes.

▶ Twenty-one thousand credit or debit card purchases are made every minute in the UK.

▶ The average household debt in the UK (excluding mortgages) is around £6,500.

▶ Australians love to gamble and research shows Aussies lose more than residents of any other country in the world, with Australian gambling losses at about AU$1,144 per resident.

THE SEVEN THINGS WE LOVE ABOUT BUYING AND SHOPPING

As part of writing this book (in 2015), I interviewed men and women in Australia, the UK and the USA about their shopping habits. Ninety-seven per cent of respondents had visited a shopping centre, shopping mall, retail high street, out-of-town retail park, discount store, factory outlet, online shopping site, TV shopping channel, internet shopping auction, garden centre, bookshop, furniture shop, DIY store, Apple iTunes Store, Amazon, eBay and/or Gumtree in the previous seven days. And I discovered that they loved the following seven things about shopping and buying.

1. GETTING A BARGAIN

Men and women in Australia, the UK and the USA said that getting a bargain was the main reason why they loved shopping and buying:

> 'I love finding small bargain items.'

> 'I love scoring a bargain.'

> 'I love it when you find a real bargain, when you are shopping for something that you need (or really want) and have been looking for for a while and you get it for a great price … a real bargain.'

2. HAVING NEW THINGS

The second reason is that we simply love having new things. New things make us feel confident, comfortable and complete.

> 'I simply love having new things, even when I don't need them.'

> 'I just love having something I didn't have before.'

> 'I go to the shops every day. I love having new things and trying new things.'

John in New York said, 'I love shopping and having new things. I feel more in style, and the confidence that comes with that. At the moment I'm buying things for my apartment, buying things makes me feel more settled'. Sue in Sydney said, 'I feel good when I have new clothes'.

3. THE EXCITEMENT

Excitement was the third reason people loved shopping. Wherever we are in the western world, we have a love affair with the excitement and buzz of shopping.

'I love the "thrill of the chase" when I go to a shop.'

'Shopping gives me a buzz.'

'The thrill and buzz of buying something new.'

'I get a buzz of excitement—and it can be addictive.'

4. SEARCHING FOR SOLUTIONS

The fourth reason is, we love searching for and getting what we need to solve a problem or to finish a project:

'The thing I love about shopping is getting something I've been searching for to solve a problem.'

'I love researching the options then going out shopping and looking for solutions.'

'I love the feeling that I'm about to finally solve the "I've got nothing to wear" problem and make my life complete by finding the perfect outfit for every occasion.'

'I love shopping and buying the most when I find and get the bit or piece needed to complete or progress a project, especially if it is an innovation or unusual solution.'

'I love the shopping "hunt": the researching, comparing and reading reviews, especially for labour-saving devices.'

5. SPECIAL TREATS

Giving ourselves, our children, our families and friends gifts and treats is the fifth reason we love shopping:

'I love watching the joy on my daughter's face when she gets something new.'

'I love the feeling of treating myself to something.'

The men and women I spoke to said they liked to buy new things as a special treat, or self-reward, to make them feel good and special. Several of my colleagues said they loved the joy of buying gifts or 'special treats' for others.

6. REPLACING SOMETHING OLD OR BROKEN

Replacing something old or broken was the sixth reason. Many people said they liked to buy new things to replace old ones, whilst others said they enjoyed replacing older items with new designs.

7. OWNING SOMETHING NO-ONE ELSE HAS

Finally, several people said that they loved buying things that were different because they liked owning things that no-one else had:

'I just love that I own things that are different to everyone else.'

'I love it when other people notice I have this new and different item.'

WHY WE SHOP AND BUY SO MUCH

On her blog 'Recovering Shopaholic', Debbie Roes, a personal development coach, explains some reasons for compulsive shopping*:

▶ Boredom—When we don't have a lot going on in life, we tend to shop more. A trip to the shopping centre provides a sense of excitement when we don't have anything to do.

▶ Avoidance—Shopping is a consuming activity that takes our minds away from other things such as family arguments, debts and problems at work.

▶ Depression—Every year, one in five Australians experiences some form of mental illness. Shopping

---

* Thank you to Debbie for kindly allowing me to summarise her ideas.

can lift our mood temporarily and provide some relief, if only for an hour.

▶ Loneliness—Social media has made it easier to connect, yet many of us suffer from loneliness. When we're shopping, we're amongst other people, and that helps many people to feel less alone.

▶ Low self-esteem and insecurity—Debbie explains that for most of her life she'd struggled with low self-esteem and feelings of not being 'good enough'. Wearing new and stylish clothes attracted compliments, which created a vicious cycle for her of constantly buying new clothes to keep up and be in fashion.

▶ Poor body image—Feeling unattractive can send us shopping in the hope that we will find 'magic' clothes that make us feel more positive about how we look.

▶ Peer pressure—For lots of people, shopping is the only fun activity they share with friends and family. It's easy to spend too much money or buy things we don't really need when we go shopping with other people.

▶ Past poverty and deprivation—Some people who shop too much do so because they've experienced childhood poverty or struggled with financial difficulties earlier in their lives.

▶ Passive aggression—Sometimes people shop to get back at a parent or spouse. Excessive shopping and large credit card debts are used to express negative feelings and displeasure.

▶ Symptom substitution—Studies show that one type of compulsive behaviour is often replaced with another, especially when the underlying reasons for the behaviour remain unresolved.

WHAT TRIGGERS SHOPPING AND BUYING?

In her book *To Buy or Not to Buy*, Dr April Benson describes the different types of shopping triggers. They include situational, cognitive, interpersonal, emotional and physical triggers.

SITUATIONAL TRIGGERS

Situation triggers are the circumstances that make us want to go shopping and buying—for example, seeing a sale sign in a shop window, buying a new outfit for a job interview or going shopping on a day off work.

COGNITIVE TRIGGERS

Cognitive triggers are the thoughts and knowledge we have that make us want to shop. For example:

▶ 'If I don't buy this now, I'll miss out.'

▶ 'I worked four hours of overtime this week, so I deserve a reward.'

▶ 'I feel guilty for arguing with my partner, so I'll buy us both a treat to apologise.'

INTERPERSONAL TRIGGERS

Interpersonal triggers relate to our relationships, communications and interactions with others. Such triggers may include buying new clothes to impress friends, going shopping when we feel undervalued at work, or going shopping after an argument with a partner or friend.

EMOTIONAL TRIGGERS

Many of us shop for emotional reasons: we feel annoyed and so we shop to forget; we feel sad and a trip to the shops boosts our mood; we feel lonely but at the shopping centre we're surrounded by people; or we're stressed with issues at work so we go shopping at lunchtime to have a happy experience.

PHYSICAL TRIGGERS

Sometimes we see shopping as a relief or break from physical issues and problems. For example:

▶ We're on a diet and an hour of shopping takes our mind off food.

▶ We've had back pain all day at work, so we go to the shops after work to buy ourselves a treat.

▶ We're waiting for medical test results and a day at the shopping mall provides a temporary distraction.

NEXT TIME YOU'RE AT THE SHOPS ...

Dr Benson suggests we ask ourselves six questions before we buy:

1   Why am I here?

2   How do I feel?

3   Do I need this?

4 What if I wait?

5 How will I pay for it?

6 Where will I put it?

MY TOP TIPS TO AVOID OVER-SHOPPING

1 Plan—Apparently 70 per cent of our purchases are unplanned. I never go food shopping without a list.

2 Be quick—The more time we spend (in minutes) in a shop, the greater our 'conversion rate'. In other words, the more likely it is that we become a buyer, not a looker. I avoid lingering. I go in and get out as fast as possible.

3 Don't touch—Retailers know that if we touch an item we're more likely to buy it. I avoid touching.

4   Bring your own music—Shops play the
     favourite music of their target audience, and
     this music makes us happy and more likely
     to stay in the shop longer. I listen to my
     own music on my smart phone instead.

5   Avoid making conversation—Like most
     people, I'm kind and I don't want to be
     rude. Retailers know that if we engage in
     conversation with their staff, we're more
     likely to buy. I say hello and politely thank
     the staff when they ask if I need help, but I
     try not to engage in a full conversation.

PART 2:
MY STORY

WHERE MY
NO-BUYING BEGAN

My 'journey' began in December 2012 on my way to India for the Mumbai leg of the BMW Guggenheim Lab.* In the airport lounge, I read an article about an Aussie family who had only bought 'things and stuff' from second-hand stores for a year.

In the run-up to Christmas, the most consumerist time of year, I spent some time in one of the poorest places on earth: Dharavi Slum, Mumbai. On the streets and in the slums of Mumbai I saw people with next to nothing who really and truly valued everything that

---

* The BMW Guggenheim Lab was a mobile and temporary town hall travelling to and resident in New York, Berlin and Mumbai in 2011 and 2012. Part urban think tank, part community centre and part public gathering space, the temporary building was used to bring people together to discuss and exchange ideas about cities of the future. (www.bmwguggenheimlab.org)

they had and owned. To be blunt, it made me feel guilty and deeply ashamed of our western world consumption.

That same week, Sarah Wilson (@_sarahwilson_) tweeted that $50 billion would be spent on gifts in Australia that Christmas, and $700 million worth of them would be in landfill by February. Minimalist Joshua Becker, of becomingminimalist.com wrote, 'While many of us search department store shelves to find the perfect gift for "someone who has everything", 768 million people do not have access to clean drinking water and 2.5 billion people live without proper sanitation'.

On New Year's Eve 2012, my friends Deanne, Julie, Declan and Gavin and I sat on the beach in Hawaii and made New Year's Resolutions. The others chose going to yoga once a week, exercising daily and leaving work on time: I announced my resolution was buying nothing new or second-hand for a year.

As I wrote in the introduction, I only lasted until the end of April. That year, I saw buying nothing as a hardship, filled with doom and gloom. Like a year of punishment. And as Rhonda Byrne says in the book *The Secret*, 'Negativity creates negativity'. I was negative and I failed—in Hastings Street, Noosa, I bought a pair of trousers which, ironically and ashamedly, I've worn less than ten times.

Last year, 2014, by contrast, I saw a year without buying as an awesome opportunity, an adventure and a whole new way of life, and I loved it. I even created some 'rules':

▶ Yes, I was allowed to buy food and absolutely essential toiletries.

▶ Yes, I could buy 'experiences'. Going to the movies, horseriding and dinners out were fine. That wasn't buying 'stuff'.

▶ I could *not* buy any new or second-hand clothes, shoes, bags, books, music, CDs, DVDs, content via iTunes, computer things, newspapers, magazines, toiletries, perfumes, bubble baths, homeware, kitchenware, bedding, towels, household items, garden things or any general 'stuff'.

MY NO-BUYING YEAR
IN TWEETS

Here's a record of how my year went, via my status updates on Twitter and Facebook.

> 1 month done, 11 to go. Last month (January) I found/received/acquired 4 pre-loved books & 2 ice cube trays (from kerbside, which I've soaked in bleach!). I politely declined, after much deliberation, 1 juicer & 1 table, in fear I'd end up as 'The Hoarder of 2014'.

> Month 2 (February) done, 10 to go. Last month I received 3 pre-loved books, 2 brand new books, 5 magazines, 1 Leadership course & 1 blogging seminar. Awesome!! And so to month 3…

Month 3 (March) done, 9 to go. Last month I received a bag of clothes from my friend & former colleague Kylie & 2 magazines from Qantas business class crew. Awesome! And so to Month 4…

Beat my Personal Best! Month 4 done, 8 left. April = found a chair, 1 book swap & received a book from @ AGAuthor. Sadly, 1 North Face fleece left on a Qantas flight. Now to Month 5.

Month 5 done, 7 left. May = nothing bought/received. Shoes 100% worn out! & savings growing. Now to Month 6

6 months done. Halfway! June = nothing purchased & 2 book swaps. Huge gratitude to my family for giving me a horse riding helmet for my birthday…. first birthday in absolutely ages when I really REALLY appreciated receiving something new…. it felt like it did at Christmas as a kid, when new things were a real treat! I'm writing a 7 step 'How to' book & 12 week online program for kicking the buying habit! Now to month 7

Month 7 done, 5 left. It's now such a part of normal life that I forgot to send an update! To Month 8…

Month 8 done. 4 months of my 'experimental living' to go! And so to Month 9…

Month 9 done. No purchases, no swaps but sold 'clutter' on Gumtree = $180! and so to Month 10…

10 MONTHS DONE!!! 2 months left… that said I want/need nothing so = life changing experience. And so to Month 11…

11 months DONE! 1 mth left. Nothing I need/want = life changing year. Now Month 12

Today (Dec 28) marks 365 days of me buying nothing new or 2nd hand for 1 year. It's been an interesting experimental year of #swapping & sharing

Since 28 December 2013 the only things I have purchased are: food, toothpaste, shampoo and Tampax

MY OLD HABITS

I wasn't a shopaholic and I didn't have huge credit card debts, but I had a few impulse shopping addictions. I love books and magazines—I read a book a month and can read a magazine cover to cover in a few hours. I found it very difficult to walk past a bookshop without being sucked in by yet another 'Buy three books for the price of two' offer. If I was at the airport or train station I always bought a magazine, whether I needed one or not.

I also had a habit of buying stuff for the house I didn't really need. I like living in a cosy home; if I saw 'the most beautiful cushion in the world' in a shop window, I'd want to buy it.

I also discovered my 'pain' points, the reasons why I went shopping and bought stuff:

▶ Boredom. It was easy to go to the shops when I had nothing better to do.

▶ Rewarding myself. I work long hours. I'd always treat myself with new clothes after a sixty-hour week.

▶ Peer pressure. Lots of my friends love shopping, and I was easily influenced into buying too.

SEVEN THINGS I LOVE ABOUT QUITTING CONSUMERISM

Last year, a newly engaged colleague bought her first house. She told me she'd be happy when they had a new kitchen and bathroom, a bigger dining table, a larger TV, a 4WD and a trailer tent.

There's plenty of research and endless books on the pursuit of happiness, and none of them suggest shopping or buying as the answer. That's why I undertook the experiment of buying nothing new or second-hand. I don't have much authority on the subject of anti-consumerism, but here's my wisdom and the seven things I love about quitting shopping and buying.

1. YOU USE UP EVERYTHING THAT YOU ALREADY HAVE

I used up what I already had. Psychotherapist Stelios Kiosses, who works with extreme hoarders, says there's a little bit of hoarder in all of us. I used to travel a lot, but even I questioned my sanity when I counted eighty-four bars of hotel soap in my bathroom cupboard. I used to use the soap during my hotel stay and then wrap it up and bring it home, because I knew the hotel cleaners would throw it away—and that's a complete waste. So I used them up, rather than buying shower gel. I also discovered twenty 5g tubes of premium-brand toothpaste lurking in the back of the cupboard! I used those up too, instead of saving them for 'later'.

2. YOU MAKE BETTER USE OF YOUR EXISTING ASSETS

I definitely made better use of my existing assets. I'm no Imelda Marcos, but like most western women, if I'm honest, I only wore 50 per cent of the clothes that I owned. So I got out the entire contents of my wardrobe at the start of my buy-nothing year—looked, pondered, sorted, rearranged and put it all back—and then I wore them all that year. And the things I really didn't like? Well, I sold them and had clothes-swapping parties with my friends.

Apparently the average American buys 67 brand-new items of clothing each year.

3. YOU SWAP AND SHARE

Why do 400 people with 400 lawns, all in the same town or suburb, each own a lawnmower?

I like sharing. I had been wanting to read a book called *Who stole my mojo?* for ages when it turned up on the share shelf at my block of flats. I read it, I gave it back and then I started swapping and sharing the books I owned with neighbours, friends and colleagues. Like Rachel Botsman says, 'We don't need to own a drill, we just want a hole in the wall'.

4. YOU HAVE MORE TIME

I had more time—and cash—to spend on awesome days out at the beach or horseriding. I learnt that lots of people spend a lot of time managing their stuff: and they were desperate to share their pain. My friend Julie told me how she'd spent her entire weekend moving the stuff she didn't use from one side of her garage to the other. My bestie Sarah emailed with tales of finally clearing out 'under the stairs', whilst my colleague Jodie told me it's her family's lifelong ambition to 'sort out and downsize all their junk'.

5. YOU VALUE WHAT YOU HAVE

I learnt to really value what I have. When I was growing up, I only got new things on birthdays and at Christmas. I got second-hand clothes from older cousins and neighbours (that was exciting and cool!). I got my first job two weeks after my thirteenth birthday, and I worked hard and saved even harder. I made lists of what I wanted, and when I had enough money saved—and only then—that item became mine. Now credit cards, debit cards, PayPass and instant credit mean anyone and everyone can have everything right now. The saving, the wanting and the waiting have gone—we get what we want when we want it, whether we want and need it or not.

Australia has the highest personal and credit card debt in the world, amounting to a staggering AU$60,000 per person.

6. YOU REALLY WANT WHAT YOU'RE WAITING FOR

We don't need much 'stuff' to be happy. My sister Louise always laughs—I've always been a bit frugal, because I've lived my life writing down what I want to buy on a 'three-month waiting list'. If I still wanted and needed said item when the three months had passed, I bought it. Nine times out of ten, however, I no longer wanted or needed it. My 'no buying' experiment really reinforced that we need very little to be happy. I learnt that if I waited one whole year for something I would really want it.

7. YOU CAN INSPIRE OTHERS

We can set a trend and inspire others. What I learnt most was that it only takes one person to get out there and be brave and try something new to inspire many others. What was once seen by my colleagues as a 'crazy' and 'alternative' venture has now encouraged them to buy less, save more and think about what they want and need.

PART 3:
STICKING POINTS AND
CHALLENGES

THE SEVEN STICKING POINTS

I believe there are seven 'sticking points' we face when trying to break addictions and habits.

1. FEAR

The first is fear. We have a culture where we fear failure. We're too scared of embarrassment and that others will laugh at us if we fail. I was worried that people would laugh at me for undertaking my lifestyle experiment of a year without buying anything new or second-hand. I learnt that it's better to try and fail (I failed first time round), than to not try at all.

2. TOO MANY CHOICES

The second reason we (Aussies, Americans and Brits) don't break our impulse shopping addictions and habit of buying 'stuff' is because we have so many—perhaps too many—choices available. We can choose where to live, where to work, where to shop, where to send our kids to school, and even where to spend Christmas. When I was growing up in the English countryside, there was one state school and everyone walked to it. From what I remember, almost all the dads worked at one of the two factories and the mums worked in whatever job was available within walking distance of home. As for Christmas, no-one dreamt of a beach vacation. You went to stay with your granny; that's just what happened. Choice has made us want to buy everything.

3. A SENSE OF ENTITLEMENT

We have developed an extraordinary sense of entitlement. Most Aussies, as an example, feel entitled to have lots of money, a fat salary, a big house plus at least one investment property, a 'free' house through our super fund and to be able to claim next to everything in our annual tax return. This entitlement obsession has led to the explosion of blame and confrontation that characterises comments in social media, tabloid press forums and consumer affairs television shows. What all this really means is that too much time is focused on arguing, being angry, whinging, whining and trying to get what we think we deserve, and too little time is spent on breaking our habits.

4. THE NEED FOR INSTANT FIXES

Fourthly, we have developed a compulsive need for 'instant fixes'. Sometimes these instant 'need-it-right-now' fixes are the right choices, but if they are done out of short-term dissatisfaction or frustration they tend to accumulate into a string of failures and more significant problems. We are so obsessed with the here and now and the next week that we don't have time to stop and sit and solve the big problems, such as loneliness and depression.

5. WE'RE TOO BUSY 'LIKING' ON FACEBOOK

Fifthly, we are too busy 'liking' on Facebook—'liking' other people's dreams from our computers and phones. It's become a hindrance. You see, Facebook and other social media platforms are great for sharing news, but they didn't help me go a year without buying anything new or second-hand.

6. EXHAUSTION

In sixth place is exhaustion. A recent survey revealed that 53 per cent of us claim to be constantly tired, with 15 per cent feeling 'exhausted'. If most of us are waking up feeling like we need another eight hours' sleep, it means we don't have the time or energy to break our habits … we're too busy counting down the hours until bedtime.

7. NAVEL-GAZING

We have developed a navel-gazing culture: we spend our time chronically analysing every twist and turn in life. We tend to over-analyse everything: what car people drive, what they wear, where they live, how much money they spend. I discovered that if I really wanted to succeed in my year without buying anything new or second-hand, I needed to stop being hypervigilant.

I acknowledge and reference the work of Dr Susan Nolen-Hoeksema, whose work at universities across the USA on over-thinking (especially choices, entitlement, instant fixes and navel-gazing) has inspired some of the content of this chapter.

SEVEN OF OUR BIGGEST CHALLENGES AND PERSONAL BATTLES

I asked men and women in Australia, the UK and the USA what they thought would be the biggest challenges or personal battles they would face if they had to quit shopping for three months. This is what they said.

1. MAKING DO WITH WHAT WE ALREADY OWN

People said that 'making do' would be their biggest challenge:

> 'The biggest challenge for me is being content and happy with [what] I have without feeling deprived.'

'I am not sure I could cope with doing without or making do with what I already own.'

'The dissatisfaction and making do with what I own now would be really hard.'

'I don't think I would have enough clothes for all of [my] needs and that would be difficult.'

Sarah in Brisbane admitted, 'I would feel tempted and deprived if I was with a friend who was shopping and buying things for themselves and I wasn't'. Jack in Los Angeles said, 'I would grow bored with the things I already have and I would feel out of style'.

2. BOREDOM

The second challenge people said they would face if they had to quit shopping is boredom. Shopping and buying is a hobby and leisure activity for many people:

'When I am bored and lonely, shopping makes me happy.'

'I would be bored. I spend my lunch breaks and weekends browsing through the shops.'

'Boredom, frustration and the lack of excitement from not being at the shops.'

'Looking on Gumtree and researching stuff on Amazon is my hobby, so I'm not sure what I would do.'

Some people identified solutions:

'I would have to find some new hobbies.'

'I would have to find something else to supplement the thrill of shopping.'

'I would need to suggest to my friends that we do something else instead of shopping!'

3. FEELING UNPREPARED

Many people felt they would be unprepared if they had to quit shopping—unprepared if things broke or needed replacing.

'Some major item would be guaranteed to break and I'm not sure we would know how to fix it.'

'The time required to find an alternative way to meet my needs would be a challenge. It would be a challenge to repair, swap or repurpose things.'

'I would feel really inconvenienced and not at all prepared.'

'The challenge would be finding practical alternatives when a genuine need to buy things arises.'

4. WILLPOWER

The fourth personal battle was willpower:

'I would be obsessing constantly that I could not shop and buy new things.'

'Remembering I couldn't duck out to instantly meet my needs.'

'Willpower to keep not buying.'

'Resisting temptation.'

'Breaking the habit of just buying something when you want it.'

5. NOT BUYING GIFTS

Not buying gifts and presents for children, families and friends was seen as the fifth challenge:

'Not being able to buy things for other people would be a real challenge.'

'Not buying things for others would be a challenge. I always put a lot of thought and planning into gifts for people.'

'Not being able to buy things and presents for family and friends.'

One of my friends said, 'Social and peer pressure, for example, not taking a present to a friend's house. I might be seen as odd or weird'.

6. FEAR OF MISSING OUT

Fear of missing out was the sixth challenge. Many people said that they might miss out on a brand-new product, a reduced price on an item or a bargain:

> 'The feeling that I am missing out because I can't have something that's new.'

7. FAILING TO MEET CHILDREN'S NEEDS

Finally, several people said that failing to meet their children's needs would be a challenge:

> 'A challenge would be not buying for my children and not giving them what they need.'

> 'I would be worried because I want to give my daughter new things and everything she wants and needs.'

> 'I would need to plan ahead for my two young boys as lots of their items tear, wear out or get too filthy to be presentable.'

PART 4:
THE SEVEN-STEP
PROCESS

THE SEVEN STEPS I TOOK
TO BREAK MY IMPULSE SHOPPING
ADDICTION & HABIT OF BUYING 'STUFF'

These are the seven steps that worked for me:

Step 1—I identified my passions and priorities

Step 2—I made a budget and sorted out my banking

Step 3—I got people in place to help

Step 4—I inspected, assessed and organised my 'stuff'

Step 5—I got into swapping, sharing and selling

Step 6—I used everything that I already had

Step 7—I got out and had fun

REALITY CHECK

Before I started the seven steps, I did a reality check. I completed the following three activities.

ACTIVITY 1

I thought about the last time I'd been on a shopping spree (at the shops or online) and then asked myself these questions:

▶ How long did my spree last?

▶ What was the day and time?

▶ How much cash and how many credit cards did I take with me?

▶ Did I take a shopping list?

▶ What did I buy?

▶ How much money did I spend?

ACTIVITY 2

I reflected on the answers from Activity 1, and then I asked myself these three questions:

▶ Were the purchases planned or unplanned?

▶ Were these purchases necessary or unnecessary?

▶ Did I spend more or less than I had planned to spend?

ACTIVITY 3

For the following week, I kept a shopping, buying and money diary (in an old notebook). I wrote down information about every single item that I bought, and the price, and recorded:

▶ the time of day that I went shopping

▶ what I went to the shops to buy

▶ why I went shopping

▶ what I actually bought and arrived home with.

I soon discovered it was very easy to go to the shops after work to buy milk, and to get home with milk, a magazine, shampoo and a bunch of flowers!

I used the list to look at the full cost of everything I'd bought, including the cleaning, organising, insuring, maintaining, fixing, replacing and removing expenses and costs.

STEP 1: I IDENTIFIED MY PASSIONS AND PRIORITIES

The first step that I took was to identify my passions and priorities.

I wanted to focus on me, not on what I owned or wanted to own, and so the first goal I set was to identify what I was passionate about and what my priorities were.

I found that admitting that buying nothing new or second-hand was possible and being grateful helped me to start the process of breaking my impulse shopping addiction and habit of buying 'stuff'. Here's what I did that worked for me.

I ADMITTED IT WAS POSSIBLE

I failed the first time I tried a year of no buying (2013). In 2014, I tried again, but this time I admitted it was possible. As I've written before, I saw 'no buying' as an exciting opportunity, an adventure and as a whole new way to live my life—a lifestyle experiment. Positive thinking creates positive experiences.

I SWITCHED OFF THE TV

Apparently we see 5,000 advertisements every day telling us to buy. Adverts are everywhere: on bus shelters, on the back of taxis, on the sides of buildings, in newspapers, on social media and on TV. Some studies indicate that American corporations spend US$50 billion every year on television advertisements to convince us to shop and buy. I couldn't avoid all advertising, but I did switch off commercial TV as much as possible. I muted the adverts and commercial breaks!

I SET MY GOALS & PRIORITIES FOR THE YEAR

I asked myself to finish this sentence:

'If I really wanted to, I could_____'

I set myself a goal to save one quarter (25 per cent) of my annual salary and to save money for one big experience, a horseriding holiday. I also created a number of smaller goals for the twelve months using the following table.

My goals for 2014			
Goal 1			
Goal 2			
Goal 3			
Jan–Mar 2014	**Apr–Jun 2014**	**Jul–Sep 2014**	**Oct–Dec 2014**
Goal 1	Goal 1	Goal 1	Goal 1
Goal 2	Goal 2	Goal 2	Goal 2
Goal 3	Goal 3	Goal 3	Goal 3

I WROTE MY 'PASSION LIST'

I answered these questions: What do I love doing? What brings me happiness? What makes me smile? What could I do all day? What are my favourite weekend activities? What don't I enjoy? I wrote my answers on my 'passion list':

I love spending time with my family and friends, reading, watching movies, massages, the beach, long country walks, riding my bicycle, horseriding and eating roast lamb.

Nothing makes me happier than a day at North Stradbroke Island walking, picnicking, surfing and talking!

I don't really like watching sport on TV, car-chase movies, seasickness or cooking.

What do you love to do? What makes you feel alive, full of energy and bursting with enthusiasm? How do you want to spend your time?

I IDENTIFIED MY SHOPPING & BUYING ISSUES

I used a number of resources on the internet, including the Wheel of Life, to identify why I had an impulse shopping addiction and habit of buying 'stuff'.

As I wrote in the chapter 'My old habits', the three main reasons I went shopping and buying were:

▶ boredom

▶ rewarding myself

▶ peer pressure.

A number of resources ask people to look at what they are grateful for and what their issues, barriers and blockages are in each area of their life, including:

creativity, finances, career, education, family, friends, physical activity, health, home environment, cooking and food, relationships, social life and spirituality. Such tools might not help everyone, but they helped me.

I MADE A 'WHY I AM NOT SHOPPING & BUYING' LIST

Instead of making a list of what I wanted to buy, I made a 'Why I am not shopping and buying' list. Things on my list included saving money and being able to afford a massage once a fortnight.

I LEARNT TO BE GRATEFUL

My mum gave me a little leather notebook for Christmas and I made this into a gratitude diary. I wrote a list of three things for which I was grateful every day, for the 365 days of 2014. I soon discovered it was the little things, not stuff, that I was most grateful for: an email from a friend in the UK, a beach walk with friends, riding my bicycle along the river and having an hour to read a book.

I GAVE MYSELF SOME REWARDS

I decided to give myself a reward at the end of each month. My rewards included things like a trip to the movies.

STEP 1: SUMMARY

The things that I found helped me to break my impulse shopping addiction and habit of buying 'stuff' without dramatically changing my life were:

▶ admitting it was possible

▶ identifying passions and issues

▶ making a 'Why I am not shopping and buying' list

▶ learning to be grateful

▶ rewarding myself.

STEP 2: I MADE A BUDGET AND SORTED OUT MY BANKING

The second step that I took was to make a budget and sort out my banking.

I set myself two goals before I started Step 2:

1   to save 25% of my net salary each month

2   to carry cash, not credit cards.

Rising living costs, credit card debts and fear of redundancy are just some of the issues facing people in the UK, the USA and Australia. The only real certainty is the amount of money we earn or receive each month, yet our 'stuff'—our electrical items, furniture, homewares and clothes—cost us money all the time. Fixing, maintaining, insuring and cleaning. I found that setting up a monthly budget and getting my banking in order helped me to break my impulse shopping addiction and habit of buying 'stuff'. Everyone's circumstances and financial obligations are different, but here are the three things that I did, that worked for me.

1. I SET UP ELEVEN BANK ACCOUNTS

First, I went to the bank and set up eleven bank accounts. The bank wasn't very happy about this, but I persuaded them to agree. When I was a child, my grandmother had three or four different jam jars where she kept cash for different household bills. Eleven accounts allowed me to replicate the jam-jar system in the digital world.

2. I SET UP A MONTHLY BUDGET

I named each of my eleven bank accounts and set a clear monthly budget for each account.

▶ Account 1 is my current account. This account accepts my monthly incomings (for example, $2,400 per month)

▶ Bank accounts 2 to 11 hold my money for each household and life expense (e.g. health insurance or car expenses).

On the day I'm paid, I transfer money into each of the ten accounts. This takes approximately eight minutes of my time.

Here's an example:

Rent/mortgage	900
Water, gas, electricity	100
Car expenses and fuel	100
Food	300
Telephone and internet	100
Health insurance	100
Health	50
Weekend activities	200
Emergencies	100
Savings	450

I transfer the money between each account and it allows me to track when I withdraw cash, what I spend, how much I spend and where I spend it.

When I was growing up, there was little money. I used to save my birthday, Christmas and pocket money for our annual family camping holiday in Cornwall. My mum would empty my money box and tell me to either divide my total savings by the number of holiday days or to choose carefully and buy the one thing I really wanted on the last day of our holiday. I once waited all week to buy a one-person inflatable boat!

3. I STOPPED USING DEBIT & CREDIT CARDS

I only carried cash. I stopped using my credit and debit cards. I locked both of my cards in a drawer (for emergency purposes only) and carried cash instead.

STEP 2: SUMMARY

The things that I found helped me to break my impulse shopping addiction and habit of buying 'stuff' without dramatically changing my life were:

▶ setting up a number of bank accounts

▶ having a clear budget

▶ putting some of my wages into a long-term savings account on the day I'm paid

▶ carrying cash, not cards.

MY TEN TOP TIPS FOR SAVING MONEY

1 Write down everything you spend for a week: everything from a $2 bottle of milk to $10 for fuel.

2 Do an audit and review of all direct debits, standing orders and monthly charges.

3 Take a shopping list when food shopping—it helps prevent impulse shopping.

4 Take out $5 less each time you withdraw cash from a bank or ATM.

5 Pay an extra $5 each month on monthly mortgage repayments.

6 Take lunch and snacks from home to work. Fewer trips to the shops mean fewer opportunities to buy.

7 Move money to a savings account on the day you get paid.

8 Save money each month for Christmas.

9 Pay with cash, not cards.

10 Break your shopping and buying habits with a thirty-day or three-month 'waiting list'.

BREAK SHOPPING AND BUYING HABITS
WITH A 30-DAY OR 3-MONTH
'WAITING LIST'

When I was a teenager, my sister Louise always laughed at me because I'd write down what I wanted to buy on a three-month 'waiting list'. If I still wanted and needed the item when the three months had passed, I'd buy it. However, nine times out of ten I no longer wanted or needed it. More often than not, I couldn't remember why I even wanted it or was excited about it in the first place. My 'no buying' experiment has really reinforced that we need very little 'stuff' to be happy.

Other people use a thirty-day list, but three months works for me.

When you discover a pair of shoes, item of clothing, book or DVD that you 'must have', would you consider putting it on a waiting list?

CHRISTMAS
IT'S ABOUT THE BRUSSELS SPROUTS, NOT THE BUYING AND SPENDING

Christmas 2005 was my best Christmas EVER. I spent the day knee-deep in mud, shared one slice of Christmas cake with my family and sang Christmas carols with complete strangers. We were travelling to the Maasai Mara in Kenya in a rusty old minivan and spent fourteen hours of Christmas Day waiting patiently to cross a flooded river. There were no presents, no decorations and no lavish commercial displays of affection. Instead my mum, dad and sister and I laughed until our bellies ached, created impromptu no-props Christmas games, celebrated uninterrupted quality time together and made memories we'll cherish forever.

In 2014, Christmas spending was set to cost each Australian AU$1,079. Research by the Commonwealth Bank forecasted that Aussies would spend $7.6 billion on gifts and $4.6 billion on Christmas holidays. Research in the USA suggested that the average

American would spend more than fifteen hours in the three weeks before Christmas shopping for gifts.

Many believe that Christmas is now more about spending money than anything else.

In the run-up to Christmas 2012, TV personality and *I Quit Sugar* author Sarah Wilson wrote, 'of the $50 billion we will spend on gifts in Australia this Christmas (2012), $700 million will be in landfill by February 2013'. More recently, she wrote, 'Australians toss $8 billion worth of edible food every year'.

Minimalist Joshua Becker wrote, 'While many of us search department store shelves to find the perfect gift for "someone who has everything", 768 million people do not have access to clean drinking water and 2.5 billion people live without proper sanitation'.

So I'm asking: Christmas. Is it about the brussels sprouts, not the buying and spending?

Yes, personally, I believe it is.

In a 2014 *Courier-Mail* article called 'Tis the season to spend up', Commonwealth bank economist Diana Mousina said, 'there were still more negative consumers than positive consumers … The majority of people are concerned that the unemployment rate will keep going up'.

… And I'm one of 'em.

Last year I was calling myself a revolutionary—just like Russell Brand!—because I was buying nothing new or second-hand for one whole year. Here are five things I did to celebrate last year's festive season.

1. PRESENCE IS THE PRESENT

I spent time, not money, with the people I love and cherish. I switched off the TV, the phone, the computer and the social media. I reconnected. I gave people my quality time. That meant helping my friend Deb with the homeless shelter soup kitchen, having listening lunches with colleagues, long beach walks with my best friends and good fun days out with my family. In today's frantically busy world, an hour of time is priceless: sharing each other's presence really is the greatest present of all.

2. RE-GIFTING

I wasn't too embarrassed to re-gift. My Great-aunt May was a serial re-gifter. Years ago it was frowned upon, but with the rise of swapping, sharing and restaurant doggie bags, anything goes. I found precious books I'd read and loved, I wrote a personal message inside and I re-gifted them to someone who'd appreciate them just as much as I did. Happiness doesn't have to be purchased in a store.

3. EXPERIENCES AND MEMORIES

It's the memories we make, not the presents we receive, that we'll remember for years to come. I gave my family, who I only see once or twice a year, experiences to treasure—not something manufactured and wrapped in plastic. I expressed my love with things they love: membership to the local lawn bowls club for my dad, movie tickets, coffee vouchers and afternoon teas after long country walks.

4. BORROWING, NOT BUYING

I borrowed and didn't buy. If I needed extra plates, cutlery or chairs, I borrowed them from neighbours. To paraphrase Moses Henry Cass, 'We do not inherit the earth from our ancestors; we borrow it from our children'. Our world's resources are limited, so from now on I'm borrowing what I need if and when I actually need it.

5. CONTENTMENT, NOT COMPARING

Everyone is on a different life journey and we all have a different story. I didn't compare our Christmas with that of others; instead, I enjoyed the one we had. Let's be content with what we own, the size of our home, the age of our car and the dynamics of our families. Sure, the Smith family had an argument—or three!—on Christmas Day, but Christmas, we know, is a celebration of being together, not about the perfect tree.

It sounds easy, right?

If we really want our Christmases to be about the brussels, not the buying, let's share each other's presence as the greatest present of all, let's not be too embarrassed to re-gift, let's give the people we love memories to treasure, let's be happy borrowing, not buying, and let us be content with everything that we are and have. That way, even if we're knee-deep in mud with only one slice of cake between four people, we'll make Christmas memories we'll cherish forever.

Do you agree?

What inspires you at Christmas?

What would you do for family and friends instead of buying gifts?

STEP 3: I GOT PEOPLE IN PLACE TO HELP

The third step that I took was to get people in place to help. I set myself two goals before I started Step 3:

1   to be part of an accountability group to keep myself accountable

2   to share my progress each month.

In a *Huffington Post* article (January 2015), Johann Hari (author of *Chasing the Scream: The first and last days of the war on drugs*) wrote, 'the opposite of addiction is not sobriety. It is human connection'. We humans have a deep desire to bond and form connections—when we can't connect with each other, we'll connect with anything else that we can find. Which might explain why, when we're feeling bored and lonely, we go shopping.

Academic research shows that people who are surrounded by people who inspire them—family, friends, teachers, elders and leaders in the community—achieve and exceed their goals. In my year of buying nothing new or second-hand, I got people in place to help me. Here's what I did. It worked.

I MET MY ACCOUNTABILITY GROUP ONCE A FORTNIGHT

I've been part of an accountability group for a year. There are six of us and we meet face-to-face over lunch once a fortnight and have Skype (or Google Hangout) meetings fortnightly in between. I also have an accountability buddy, Cheryl. We keep in touch every one to seven days by phone, text message, email or Skype. We keep each other progressing, staying on track, and we help each other when we're feeling down, low and fed up.

Here are my recommendations on what to do at an accountability meeting:

▶ Choose a leader. Someone who'll track the group's progress and remind people to check in between meetings.

▶ Review the top five things that everyone did and achieved in the previous fortnight.

▶ Discuss the problems, successes and failures that everyone is experiencing.

▶ Set a list of three or four actions to be achieved before the next meeting.

I MET UP WITH PEOPLE DOING SIMILAR PROJECTS

I met up with people doing similar projects by going to as many free events, seminars and talks as possible. I went to events about minimalism, living with less and saving money. I got to talk to people doing similar experiments, and it made me feel normal, not a freak!

I JOINED MEETUP.COM AND SOCIAL MEDIA GROUPS

I joined a heap of Facebook groups and meet-up groups (via www.meetup.com) that were about being minimalist and buying less, to keep me inspired and motivated.

I SHARED MY PROGRESS EVERY MONTH

Each month I shared my progress with family, friends, colleagues, followers and absolute strangers on Facebook, Twitter and LinkedIn. It inspired me to continue.

STEP 3: SUMMARY

Here are the two things that I found helped me to break my impulse shopping addiction and buying 'stuff' habit without dramatically changing my life:

- ▶ being accountable to myself and others
- ▶ sharing my progress once a month.

CAN KARAOKE IN OUR CITY PARKS TRANSFORM OUR SPENDING HABITS?

When my colleague Jing suggested karaoke for a team social event, there were gasps of despair. Our manager hastily booked lanes at the local tenpin bowling alley.

On the other side of the world, in a not-so-pristine park in Berlin, an Irish guy called Joe draws crowds of more than 3,000 people to his Bearpit Karaoke… and that's before the karaoke has even begun. Which got me thinking, can karaoke in our city parks transform our spending habits?

It seems an odd thing to say, but yes, I believe it probably can. Councils, government agencies and marketing bureaus across the globe strive to find ways to get people into our town and city centres. Some spend millions on extravagant firework spectaculars, whilst others book international music acts or have an almost continual stream of farmers' markets and craft fairs, many of which seem to fail to deliver the desired *je ne sais quoi*.

When my trusted Lonely Planet guidebook told me that Bearpit Karaoke was a must-see on a Sunday afternoon in Berlin, I couldn't resist investigating! I arrived at Mauerpark amazed at the activity. The flea market was in full swing, with hundreds of people buying and selling old bikes, vintage clothes and 'maker movement' crafts. People young and old relaxed on the unkempt grass, surrounded by complimentary entertainment from skateboard tricksters, circus performers and wannabe rock stars. In the stone amphitheatre, a contortionist was pleasing a small but happy audience.

As I sat watching and waiting, it became apparent that something big was about to go down. Within minutes, the crowd of a hundred or so had swelled to at least a thousand—families, locals, students and tourists—and in less than half an hour it was standing-room only. The contortionist took her final bow, and the crowd broke into rapturous applause as a scruffy-looking guy in a checked shirt and baseball cap walked across the stage. This was it. Joe Hatchiban had arrived and my opinion of karaoke was about to be changed.

Since the winter of 2009, Joe has been using portable, battery-powered boxes on a 'hacked' cargo bike to help people unleash their inner *Rampensau* (limelight hog) on Sundays. Weather permitting, Joe fetches up around 3 pm and invites anybody who so wishes to take the stage for a few minutes, to show those gathered what they can do with a backing track and a microphone. Joe has shown that with no budget, a very large serve of motivation, Facebook and people's desire to get involved, you really can transform a public space.

Bottom-up approaches like this are changing patterns of activity in our towns and cities.

Without a shadow of a doubt, Ottery St Mary, a chocolate-box village in rural Devon in the UK, puts life first. Each and every year on Guy Fawkes Night, locals run through their narrow streets brandishing burning barrels. Those who have visited Ottery on November 5th know that perpetuating a tradition is the objective and commercial considerations take second place: as the website says, 'if you attend it, don't try and change it, just stand back and enjoy'.

I admit, when you're there in the crowd with 20,000 others and a very large ball of fire is coming right toward you, it's hard to understand what motivates men, women and children into putting a full-sized lit tar barrel on their shoulders and then running down the street. But what I do know is that these brave folks are accepting complete strangers into their town to enjoy an exhilarating and risky spectacle. Of course it's deemed dangerous, but good organisation, cooperation between the various agencies involved and people using good old-fashioned common sense manages the risk. And: it's totally free.

Here in Brisbane, Amy Saunders, who I co-founded the cycling group Lazy Sunday Cycle (www.lazysundaycycle.com) with, is passionate about encouraging interactions between people of different generations, cultural and socio-economic backgrounds. Amy founded Games Night at King George Square to help break down barriers in society—on the last Thursday of every month, in a public square in the Brisbane CBD, giant board games can be played by anyone and with anyone. Like Joe, Amy doesn't have a big budget, but what she does have is proven knowledge that people crave interaction and a desire to be part of something fun. I guess that's why, with the help of social media, more than 300 people attend each and every event.

These stories provide a basis for taking action—though please don't run down your road with a burning barrel!—by demonstrating that low-cost activities in our towns and cities can help to support us in breaking our shopping habits, with positive benefits for individuals.

Creating and maintaining activities costs money and the economic merits are regularly called into question. If we really want our towns and cities to change, we need to learn from people like Joe, Amy and the Ottery barrel-rollers. But most of all we need to embrace the new movement of 'bottom-up self-organisation'.

The reason that people turn up every week for Bearpit Karaoke isn't because they don't have access to iTunes. It's because they want the buzz of being part of something fun, the supportive applause that comes from peer-to-peer performances, the serendipitous connections with people they wouldn't normally meet. I guess that's why karaoke has the potential to transform our spending habits.

STEP 4: I INSPECTED, ASSESSED & ORGANISED MY STUFF

The fourth step that I took was to inspect, assess and organise all the stuff in my house.

I was determined to sort out my wardrobe first, so I set myself three goals before I started Step 4:

1   to assess everything in my wardrobe

2   to wear the clothes I already owned

3   to swap and donate the clothes I didn't like.

We all love getting a bargain, having new things and treating ourselves to new clothes. Yet most of us give ourselves a really hard time about our out-of-control credit card debts, the money we've 'wasted' on clothes we never wear and the cash we've spent on things that clutter our garages and spare bedrooms. Like everyone, I felt guilty, and so I decided to inspect, assess and organise everything I owned. The contents of some drawers and cupboards were inspected, assessed and organised in less than ten minutes, while other rooms took a couple of days to complete, but the process remained the same.

1. I CREATED A SYSTEM

The first thing that I did was to create a simple system. I got six cardboard boxes and labelled them as follows:

- ▶ Box 1: Keep and use
- ▶ Box 2: Donate to charity
- ▶ Box 3: Relocate (I gave pens from conferences to a local school and soaps and toothpastes to a homeless charity)
- ▶ Box 4: Swap or share
- ▶ Box 5: Sell
- ▶ Box 6: Recycling bin or rubbish bin

2. I INSPECTED EVERY ROOM IN MY HOME

I inspected every single room in my house. No item was overlooked.

▶ In the bedroom, I'd been given new bed sheets the previous Christmas, before I'd worn out the old ones. It had been easy to ask for stuff I didn't really need.

▶ In the bathroom, I found several half-used bottles and endless free samples under the sink. I now get a cheap thrill out of using the last of something.

▶ In the kitchen—I had thirty mugs. They're now at a community centre and being put to good use. I realised the kitchen is a place it's easy to buy new things for.

▶ At my desk, I culled my pens—I now have five. I realised that buying pens and paper had been a habit, too.

3. I ASSESSED EVERY SINGLE ITEM

With every item in every room, I asked myself these questions:

▶ Do I love it?

▶ Do I use it?

▶ Does it work?

▶ If I were going to buy this item right now, how much would I pay for it?

▶ If I sold this now, how much could I sell it for?

After I'd answered these questions, I put the item in one of my six boxes.

A NOTE ABOUT SELLING THINGS

Selling unwanted and unused stuff is symbolic. I spent hours selling things online. I'm certain that the next time I go to buy something new I'll remember the night I stayed up until 2 am posting stuff on Gumtree and eBay. Yes, I felt guilty about the things I'd accumulated that I didn't need.

4. I INSPECTED MY WARDROBE, IN PARTICULAR, WITH A FINE-TOOTH COMB

Studies say if we've not worn something in two years, we're never going to wear it; they also say that we all wear the same eleven outfits week after week.

Like most western women, if I was honest, I only wore 50 per cent of the clothes that I owned. So I got everything out—the entire contents of my wardrobe, that is—and looked, pondered, sorted and rearranged. Organising my wardrobe didn't mean going to the shops to buy new things!

Here's what I did:

1   I made a vision board about my ideal wardrobe: the clothes, brands and colours I love.

2   I took photos of my favourite clothes, the items I wore the most and the things I loves wearing.

3   I made a pile of the clothes that made me feel happy.

4   I put the clothes I wore every week on hangers.

5   I set aside the clothes I didn't wear because they needed a simple repair, like a new button. A repair is cheaper than buying new.

6   I looked for clothes that could be upcycled. Simple DIY projects saved me money.

7   I scored everything on a scale of one to ten. Anything less than a seven went.

Then, I created five favourite work outfits and four weekend outfits that I love. I've promised to wear these clothes until they're worn out.

5. I GOT ORGANISED

Last, I organised the things that were left. I didn't buy any new storage items, though: I used the plastic containers and shoe boxes I already had. I stuck labels on the side of each box detailing the contents.

THREE COMMON MISTAKES

Three mistakes I made seem near-universal when you're decluttering:

1   Thinking that if I had a limited wardrobe my clothes would be boring. I actually discovered that I'd kept the clothes I really liked and loved to wear, and donated or sold the clothes that were too small, too big or a mistake purchase and I never wore.

2   Thinking that if I got rid of something, I would regret it later. I found that I didn't use, like or need most of the things I had stuffed in the back of cupboards 'just in case'.

3   Thinking that it was going to take hours of my precious time. I didn't make a to-do list. I picked small projects, got stuck in and got them finished as quickly as possible. I found that it was easier to tackle one kitchen drawer for five minutes before work than to tackle a whole room. I accomplished lots of little things rather than one big thing.

SOME CHARITIES I DONATED MY THINGS TO

My local charity shop is currently overwhelmed with 'stuff'—their storage room is packed full. So, I spent some time looking for charities and organisations that really needed my stuff:

▶ Clothes—As well as giving some preloved clothes to my local Lifeline op shop (charity shop), I gave all the T-shirts I'd received from charity walks and sports events to the Brisbane Motorcycle Street Feed for the Homeless. They feed more than 100 homeless men and women in Brisbane every Tuesday night.

▶ Bras—The Uplift Project collects new and second-hand bras and sends them to women in disadvantaged communities, where a bra is often unobtainable or unaffordable (upliftbras.org).

▶ USB sticks—I had more than twenty USB sticks from conferences: I donated them to a homeless shelter. Young men and women use them to store scanned copies of their personal documents.

I also registered lots of items for donation on Givit (givit.org.au), a charity established in 2009 that facilitates the transfer of goods to those who are vulnerable or marginalised in a safe and confidential manner. They list requests for items from charities around Australia.

STEP 4: SUMMARY

The things that I found helped me to break my impulse shopping addiction and buying 'stuff' habit without dramatically changing my life were:

▶ setting up a simple system

▶ inspecting everything

▶ asking myself some tough questions

▶ donating things to people who really needed them.

STEP 5: I GOT INTO SWAPPING, SHARING AND SELLING

The fifth step that I took was to swap, share and sell. I set myself three goals before I started Step 6:

1   to swap the clothes I didn't wear

2   to share with neighbours and friends

3   to sell the things that I no longer used.

Forty, thirty, even twenty years ago, most homes probably had just one television, one telephone and one radio. Today, most homes have a television, telephone and music system in every room. I realised that I had lots of things in my house that I didn't like and didn't use, and that I was happy to swap, share and sell. This is what I did.

I SWAPPED THE CLOTHES I DIDN'T LIKE AND DIDN'T WEAR

I swapped the clothes I didn't like and didn't wear.

Edda Hamar dreams of a world in which people choose sustainable fashion. She tells people to take their clothes off and she loves to high-five complete strangers. I'm passionate about cutting traffic congestion, I dream of a world with floating bikeways made out of waste plastic and old Coke cans and I was buying nothing new or second-hand for a year. We met at TEDxKurilpa in February 2014 rehearsing our TED talks and discovered shared passions: clothes, sharing, talking and meeting new people. And we set ourselves a challenge: to host the world's largest clothes-swapping party within fifty-six days of our first meeting.

The first event was postponed due to severe thunderstorms, but with the help of lots of other incredible people, we did hold a clothes-swapping party last year (indoors!).

MY 'HOW TO HAVE A CLOTHES-SWAPPING PARTY' GUIDE

Here's how it works for men and women attending a clothes-swapping party:

- Bring clothes that you wish to swap on clothes hangers.

- Clothes for swapping must be clean, ironed, unstained and undamaged.

- One item of clothing on a clothes hanger = one token.

- Ten items of clothing on ten clothes hangers = ten tokens.

- Enter the clothes-swapping area and choose clothes that you like.

- You can choose one piece of clothing for every token you have.

My top tip for clothes-swapping parties is that it's best to avoid swapping lingerie, socks, swimwear and shoes. Women's and men's clothes, kids' and baby clothes, and handbags are all fine.

Here's how the clothes-swapping party process works from an organiser's perspective:

► People arrive.

► They pass Checkpoint 1, where volunteers check that the clothes are clean, ironed, unstained and undamaged.

► Tokens are allocated, one per item of clothing.

► Volunteer runners take the 'checked-in' clothes to the clothes rails.

► People choose the clothes they want.

► They take the clothes they've selected to the exit area.

► They pass Checkpoint 2, where volunteers count the clothes and take the tokens from the person.

► People exit.

► Any clothes left over are donated to charity.

I SHARED THE BOOKS I'D ALREADY READ

A book I'd always wanted to read, *Who stole my mojo?*, turned up on the share shelf at my block of units last year. I struck lucky. Since that day I've put all the books and magazines that I've read and loved on the share shelf, so that my neighbours can be lucky too.

You may not have a share shelf in your building like I do, or be aware of ways you can share various possessions in your area. TuShare can be a great place to start. 1 Million Women has partnered with TuShare for the 1 Million Kilogram Challenge, to help women get and give things away for free: www.tushare. com/1millionwomen.

I SOLD SOME THINGS I DIDN'T LIKE AND DIDN'T USE

I sold some 'clutter'—unworn clothes, unwanted gifts and excess stuff—on Gumtree and made $180 in one week. I kept a list of each item I sold and how much I sold it for, to keep account of how much the stuff I had sitting in cupboards had cost me.

I'd been spending time and money storing, insuring, cleaning and sometimes fixing and maintaining things I didn't like and didn't use.

STEP 5: SUMMARY

The things that I found helped me to break my impulse shopping addiction and buying 'stuff' habit without dramatically changing my life were:

▶ swapping clothes

▶ helping to host a clothes-swapping party

▶ selling the things I didn't like and didn't use that were costing me money.

ARE 'NOT SHOPS' THE FUTURE?

In 2014, ABC News in Australia reported that ten million people in the USA were unemployed. Forty per cent of those people had been unemployed for more than six months. Ten million is a huge number to grasp, until you think of it like this—Australia has a population of twenty-three million people. Imagine every other person being out of work.

The story featured Janice, a former government worker, who was supporting her two young children as well as her niece and nephew. Her kids wanted new toys and books, but the little money she got from welfare benefits and family support was spent on essentials like rent and food.

It got me thinking: are 'shops that are not shops' the future?

My favourite city is Berlin, and in my former neighbourhood Prenzlauer Berg was Leila—a 'shop that was not a shop'. It was divided into two parts: things that were free, and things that you could borrow. The project initiator and 'shopkeeper', Nikolai Wolfert, once gave me a tour of the store. According to him, the average western home has more than 10,000 items of 'stuff'! Nikolai is passionate about sharing, trust and creating good relationships in our communities. Ultimately, he wants to help change consumer behaviour. He's also a huge fan of Sydney's Rachel Botsman, the leading advocate in what's called 'collaborative consumption', and whose book, *What's Mine is Yours*, I recently borrowed from my friend Bronwyn's friend Sam.

The free section of the shop is filled with things that people in the neighbourhood no longer need or don't really have space for. Books, CDs, DVDs, china, cutlery, trinkets, clothes, shoes, bags, garden seeds and even welly boots adorn homemade shelves—you name it and it's there! You can basically go in and take it, but only if you really need it.

The second section is dedicated to borrowing. There are two whole rooms of amazing stuff that people in the community have donated for others to use free of charge and then give back. It's the ultimate in creating a resilient community and being good neighbours. You can borrow almost anything: musical instruments, dining-room chairs, camping equipment, gardening tools, outdoor furniture, yoga mats, skateboards, children's toys, kids' books, cookery books, suitcases, hairdryers, irons and ironing boards, cots, baby change tables, rice cookers, blenders, saucepans, blankets, children's car seats, bikes, cycling helmets, barbecues, picnic baskets, car tools and DIY books. You can even borrow gardening overalls!

I'll confess, the day I first visited I felt a fraud. I had just had to go and buy a clothes airer from a department store, after several days of trawling around the second-hand stores and the flea market without success. I felt a bit embarrassed and ashamed of my shiny, plastic-wrapped new purchase at first, but I left the 'shop' feeling happy—because I'd agreed to donate my airer to Leila when I left Berlin.

Normalising borrowing is going to be a long journey. When Prince Charles talked of his environmentally friendly lifestyle—recycling old curtains into cushion covers—it was scoffed at by the media as 'penny pinching'. It's not our fault: for years, the marketing, advertising and PR agencies have told us we can have it all, and so now most of us want it all.

But things *are* changing. British chain Marks & Spencer offers customers discounts in exchange for unwanted clothes, which are then donated to Oxfam.

In Sydney, meanwhile, apparently more than 7,500 sellers take part in the annual 'Garage Sale Trail', an event to promote community recycling of unwanted stuff … and yes, most people took part because they wanted to declutter their homes.

These stories, and what I saw at Leila, show that sharing, borrowing, lending, making and mending might just be the future of 'shopping' in these times of global austerity. I reckon Janice would agree. What do you think?

STEP 6: I USED EVERYTHING THAT I ALREADY HAD

The sixth step that I took was to use everything that I already had. I set myself two goals before I started Step 6:

1   to use up all the soap, shampoo and toiletries that I already had at home

2   to wear out my clothes and shoes.

Lots of men and women in the UK, USA and Australia told me that they would feel unprepared if they quit shopping for three months—it was one of the biggest challenges discussed in Part 3. They said they would feel unprepared if things broke or needed replacing.

During my year of buying nothing new or second-hand, though, I realised I didn't actually need to buy anything new or second-hand. I just needed to use everything that I already had.

Step 6 was very simple. I used up everything that I already had:

▶ I used up all my soaps, shampoos, conditioners and moisturisers.

▶ I used the sample sachets, the travel-size bottles and all the complimentary products I had received from magazines, shops and hotels.

▶ I wore out all the shoes I had—I wore my shoes until they had holes in the soles!

▶ I used bathroom towels and tea towels until they had holes in them.

▶ I used saucepans until the handles fell off ... and then I used them without handles. (I'm still using them.)

▶ I read the magazines I already had from cover to cover and then I gave them to others.

▶ I read the books I had bought but had not read.

▶ I used scrap paper for food shopping lists.

And then, I calculated the costs and the savings. Here are two examples.

If you remember, I found eighty-four bars of hotel soap lurking in the back of my bathroom cupboard. Normally, I'd buy expensive, organic, 'free of this and free of that' shower gel at $15.99 a bottle. And I'd buy around twelve bottles a year. That's $191.88 a year. By using the soap I had, I saved almost $200.

I also got all of my books off my bookcase and sorted them into three categories:

1   books I'd read and I wanted to keep

2   books I'd not read but I wanted to read

3   books I'd not read and probably wouldn't ever read, and that I was happy to swap, share and sell.

I found forty-nine books that I had not read. Based on reading one book per month, that was two years worth of reading. The average cost of a book in Australia is AU$15 (new or second-hand), so by reading the books I already had, I saved myself $735.

By using the soap I had lurking in the bathroom cupboard, instead of buying shower gel, and by reading the books I already had sitting on my bookshelf at home, I saved myself almost $1,000.

STEP 6: SUMMARY

The things that I found helped me to break my impulse shopping addiction and buying 'stuff' habit without dramatically changing my life were:

▶ using everything that I already had

▶ calculating the costs and the savings.

CAN CUPCAKES MAINSTREAM SHARING?

When Kirsty, my sister's sister-in-law, arrived at Christmas with cupcakes in jam jars exquisitely wrapped, we knew she had a product worth developing … and eating! Like many of us, Kirsty has a dream to spend her working week doing what she is truly passionate about. Regrettably, mega-corporations, the big banks and a global recession have created in us a fear of losing a steady salary, a perception of risk and an anxiety towards change. So, could sharing capture the spirit of doing things differently and ignite that creative fire in our bellies?

Yes, I think it can. When Rachel Botsman, author of *What's Mine is Yours*, said 'we don't need to own a drill, we just want a hole in the wall', her words resonated with most people I know who read her book.

Of course, sharing is nothing new. When I was growing up, people were always knocking on our door asking to borrow my dad's cement mixer, and hardly a week passed without someone going into my mum's haberdashery shop wanting her to fix up their botched sewing project. Sharing just happens in country towns. But how do we facilitate sharing in the anonymity of the city?

'Collaborative consumption' is about sharing, trading and renting rather than owning. Enabled by technology, we can access all sorts of assets, from houses to technical skills—with global marketplaces like eBay through to peer-to-peer holiday rental services (such as AirBnB) or revolutionary concepts such as private car advertising platforms (like Motize). It has changed what we need, buy and use. But I don't think sharing is brave enough. We need to push the boundaries, and that's where Kirsty and her cupcakes come in.

Kirsty can't afford to start her own business. The council won't let her use her own kitchen, retrofitting a domestic kitchen is unviable and commercial spaces are too big and expensive. So what can people like you and me and Kirsty do in our cities to make sharing mainstream?

For a start, we can share commercial space. Most cafes where I live close on a Saturday and don't reopen until Monday. Even though they're closed, they still have the bills to pay: rent, insurance, electricity, and so the list rumbles on. So why don't we share our commercial spaces? We could give people like Kirsty 'a fair go'. Wouldn't it be ingenious if Kirsty could 'borrow' a cafe, closed on Sundays, to make her cupcakes and realise her dream?

We could share our cars. Apparently, the average car is parked for 95 per cent of its lifetime and 70 per cent of traffic in our city centres are vehicles searching for a parking spot. Whether you believe these statistics or not, the truth is that our cars cost us money when they are moving and even more when they're lying idle. That's why BMW created 'Drive Now', the first car-sharing scheme with premium cars, based on instant access and devoid of fixed pick-up/drop-off locations. BMW, and others, allow 'us' to get a car when and where we need it. I admit it's not always easy. I once shared my friend Nigel's car with my friend Roger. Sharing between friends requires planning and a fair amount of patience!

What I'm getting to here is that we can share our 'stuff'. When you live in a rented apartment like me, space is at a premium, but that's outweighed by the shared benefits—the swimming pool and the gym. In her book *The Overspent American: why we want what we don't need*, Juliet Schor explores how buying, owning and 'keeping up with the Joneses' has defined our lives. I dream of a 'man shed in every suburb', a place where we share tools, belongings and skills. Sharing creates friendships and friends form resilient communities.

If we really want sharing to be mainstream, we have to think differently.

These stories provide a prompt for change, but for habitual change our city planners need to change planning laws, our stores need to focus on access as well as selling, and we need to focus on use rather than owning. Voluntary simplicity (sharing and renting) lets me spend my time and money on things I really love (horseriding, beach days and surfing), because that's what life is all about. Tim Smit, the founder of the Eden Project, always says, 'Greatness comes from enabling people to think an idea is theirs'. With that, I'll leave you with an open invitation to help Kirsty trial her dream business.

STEP 7: I GOT OUT AND HAD FUN

The seventh step that I took was to get out and have fun. I set myself two goals before I started Step 7:

1   to participate in at least two horseriding dressage competitions in 2014

2   to go to the beach at least once a month.

When we're feeling bored, lonely, depressed or stressed, we're tempted to go shopping. I found that getting out and having more fun solved the problem. In my year of buying nothing new or second-hand, I was able to pursue and enjoy the things that are really important to me, because I wasn't bogged down with shopping, buying and repaying my credit card. For me, this meant that I've been able to write a book, study part-time, spend more time with my family and friends, go to the beach, go horseriding and have more fun! This is what worked for me.

1. I CREATED NEW HABITS

I created new habits that didn't involve shopping centres. Many psychologists and social commentators say to create a new habit you need to do the new habit every day or not at all. I created a few new and simple habits that kept me away from shops:

▶ I went to the local produce shop around the corner to avoid big supermarkets and impulse buying.

▶ I listened to TED Talks on my way to work. This meant I didn't look in shop windows.

▶ I stayed off social media and the internet until lunchtime (except for work purposes).

▶ I wrote in my gratitude diary every night before bed.

In his book *Why Clever People Do Dumb Things*, psychologist Lindsay Spencer-Matthews (greatchangemaker.

com.au) explores some of the basic drivers that make people do things they later regret. Lindsay argues that most people suffer under the illusion that they are in control of what they do, and it's incredibly common for people to understand that they're doing things that aren't helpful for them.

Lindsay says that we learn the habits of shopping accidentally during our entire lives: we're trained in those habits by observing our parents, friends, aspirational groups and avoidance groups. Lindsay's identified that most people find life has its challenges, but that our desire to change is often thwarted by our greatest enemy—our invisible automatic programming. Our 'programming' essentially results in habitual, emotional and automatic behaviour, which rules our business and personal lives and our thoughts and reactions. Lindsay commented about my year of not buying:

> 'It's common for people to look upon what Rachel was doing with humour or disbelief. It is almost certain that some people were a little threatened and even a little angry ... Rachel's one-year journey into the world of not buying is a heartening and inspiring glimpse into what a strong minded person might achieve if they really put their "minds" into action.'

2. I FOCUSED ON EXPERIENCES, NOT 'STUFF'

I spent 2014 focusing on experiences and not on shopping. I really wanted to join a book club, go to yoga once a week and walk along the Brisbane river every morning before work. But while I didn't have time to do those things, I did:

▶ go horseriding every Wednesday evening—I met new people, made new friends and had heaps of fun

▶ go to Pilates on a Thursday night for eight weeks

▶ go for a massage or reflexology once a month.

3. I MADE SOME SPECIAL INVESTMENTS

Buying nothing new or second-hand for a year meant that I had money to spend on 'special investments'. I enrolled in the Key Person of Influence 40 Week Brand Accelerator course and I self-funded my first book, *Decongestion: 7 steps for Mayors and other City Leaders to cut traffic congestion without the expense of new roads and annoyed residents* (www.cyclingrachelsmith.com/book-decongestion) with Michael Hanrahan Publishing. I would never, ever have been able to afford to invest in self-education and self-publishing if I had been impulse shopping and buying 'stuff'.

4. I PARTICIPATED IN MY LOCAL COMMUNITY

Almost five years ago, I co-founded Lazy Sunday Cycle with my friend Amy. It's all about getting normal people in normal clothes having a go at riding a bicycle for fun. It started out well, with lots of people participating. Move forward four months and we had 500 likes on Facebook—but no-one at the actual bike rides! Rather than cancel the rides and give it up as a failed experiment, we decided to have a barbecue or picnic lunch after each ride. People came, they cycled, they ate and they made friends. We all crave human connections and friendships.

Last year, I participated in my community a little bit more. I helped at community events and did some volunteering. I created a few new friendships and the local community activities kept me away from the shops.

STEP 7: SUMMARY

The things that I found helped me to break my impulse shopping addiction and buying 'stuff' habit without dramatically changing my life were:

▶ creating some new daily habits that didn't involve shops

▶ focusing on experiences

▶ making some special investments

▶ participating in the local community.

IS BUYING A SIGN OF LONELINESS?

My across-the-road neighbours Allan and Jayne*, both recently divorced and each with a prestigious city career, spend all weekend, every weekend shopping, alone. The latest gadgets, designer clothes and 'occasional' furniture (the 'just in case' stuff you sometimes need!) occupy their time and their money. Their lives are a constant cycle of researching what's bigger or better, scouring shopping malls, buying things to impress people they don't even like and throwing out the old to make way for the new.

They're not alone.

My colleague Carol, a single mum with teenage kids, told me that she goes to the shopping centre every Saturday afternoon without fail, regardless of whether she needs to buy things or not. 'It's a habit,' she says, 'an addiction, a way of life and the only thing I do'.

Some researchers believe that loneliness is twice as deadly as obesity.

---

* All names have been changed to protect people's privacy.

▶ Studies in 2013 and 2014 by the charity Independent Age revealed that severe loneliness is rife amongst young adults and over-50s.

▶ Twenty per cent of older people report that the television is their main source of company.

▶ A survey by Boston College found that people with a net worth of $78 million felt lonely.

The television, celebrating material aspiration and our obsession with fame and wealth, enables us to stay at home and reinforces the desire to buy and shop instead of pursuing passions and hobbies. It's likely to be part of the reason why more than one-fifth of kids in Britain say they 'just want to be rich'.

Is buying a sign of loneliness?

Yes, I think it probably is.

Mid-way through my year of buying nothing new or second-hand, I discovered there was absolutely nothing that I wanted, desired or needed. I valued days out and quality time with my family and friends much more than shiny shopping mall 'stuff', and it strengthened my lifelong belief that I don't need material items to be happy—less really is so much more.

Nothing makes me happier than a day at North Stradbroke Island walking, picnicking, surfing and talking!

So what can we do to quit buying and stamp out loneliness? Here are some ideas.

LET'S DISCOVER WHAT'S ON OUR DOORSTEP WITH FRIENDS WE DON'T YET KNOW

A couple of years ago my mate Jon Giles created Style Over Speed. Three or four times a year on a Friday night, a hundred or so people get dressed up—think fine dresses and dinner suits—and cycle around the Brisbane city centre. They discover what's on their own doorstep (public spaces, cafes and bars), make new friends and have a lot of fun for free.

LET'S PLAY, FOR FREE, WITH STRANGERS

Games Night at King George Square has proven that people crave interaction and a desire to be part of something fun. I think that's why, with the help of social media, several hundred people turn up each month.

LET'S 'SHOW UP' AND GET INVOLVED

Bearpit Karaoke has shown us that the real reason that people show up every Sunday afternoon is because they want the buzz of being part of something fun, the supportive applause that comes from peer-to-peer performances and the serendipitous connections with people they wouldn't normally meet.

It all sounds easy, right?

If we really want to quit buying and lessen the epidemic of loneliness, we need to stop searching for the bigger or better. We need to end the cycle of buying things to impress people we don't know or like and put an end to throwing out the 'old' to make way for the new. Let's switch off the TV, get outside and focus on things more interesting. Let's focus on people, not products, let's 'love people and use things', not the other way around, and let's embrace the things in our towns and cities that are free. And finally, let's not educate our children to be rich—instead, let's educate them to be happy, so that when they grow up they'll know the value of things, not the price.

Do you agree?

What inspires you?

What excellent free events have you seen?

IF YOU KNEW YOU WOULDN'T FAIL, WHAT WOULD YOU DO?

I was able to break my impulse shopping addictions and buying 'stuff' habits without dramatically changing my life by: identifying my passions and priorities; making a budget and sorting out my banking; getting people in place to help; inspecting, assessing and organising my 'stuff'; swapping, sharing and selling; using everything that I already had; and getting out and having more fun.

For me, the results of implementing the seven steps in this book were:

▶ being Underspent

- breaking my impulse shopping addiction and habit of buying 'stuff'
- saving 38 per cent of my net (take-home) annual salary
- being much happier and more content.

I wrote this book because I wanted to share the tools that worked for me with other people. All I can say now is, try it and see!

I'd welcome a warm introduction to your friends, family and colleagues who have an impulse shopping addiction and buying 'stuff' habit. It's my big dream that these men and women will read and implement one, some or all of the steps in this book, because the future belongs to those who believe in the beauty of being Underspent—and the reality that none of us will have an impulse shopping addiction or buying 'stuff' habit ever again.

Here's to being Underspent!

Rachel

WHERE I AM NOW
AND MY NEW HABITS

It's now three months since my year of no-buying ended. Buying nothing new or second-hand in 2014 changed my life:

▶ I broke my shopping addiction and buying habit.

▶ I feel happier, more content and very pleased to have 38 per cent of my salary sitting in the bank.

▶ I feel guilty and embarrassed about the money I've spent over the last 20 years on things I didn't like and I didn't use.

I'll be honest. I've been to the shops. In the first three months of 2015 I've bought three pairs of shoes, two books, a jumper and a handbag. I needed the shoes. I'd spent the final months of 2014 wearing my colleagues' 'spare' shoes and I'd glued the sole to the bottom of my trainers more than ten times.

The handbag and jumper were a reward for buying nothing the previous year. I'm not even sure why I bought either, but I did. As for the books ... It was a two-for-one at the airport bookshop. What more can I say!

I've had my 'spending splurge'. It didn't make me feel happy, excited or content. I probably won't be buying anything for the rest of this year.

... And yes, I do feel a little bit guilty now if I go to a shop.

THANK YOU

Writing a book (*Decongestion*) and this ebook (*Underspent*) in ten months whilst working full-time and studying has been an epic experience. Thank you to everyone who came on the journey with me and who helped and supported me. There are too many of you to name individually, but I know who you are.

Thank you to everyone who agreed to be interviewed about their shopping and buying habits. Your time and honest responses were fundamental to this book, and for that I am very grateful.

Special thanks to Andrew Griffiths, a best-selling author, who told me that everyone has at least one book inside them. Thanks, Andrew, for your guidance and encouragement. Thanks to Glen Carlson and everyone at, and doing, the Key Person of Influence (KPI) program. I could not have done any of this without your knowledge, insights and support.

Thank you to Michael Hanrahan for your brilliant book production expertise. As a first-time author I really could not have produced my first book, *Decongestion*, without you, and that knowledge has enabled me to write this ebook.

Thank you to Vanessa Battersby for editing, book production and cover design.

Thanks to my sister Louise for proofreading and being brutally honest. Thank you also to Jaclyn Sheriff for proofreading.

Last and by no means least, thank you to my family and friends, especially my Mum and Dad, Louise, Joe, Tony, Sarah and Julie. It's fair to say that without my family and friends encouraging me to plough on and never give up, I might never have got to the finish line.

FREE GIFT

Thank you for reading *Underspent*. I have a free gift for all readers—please email me at Rachel@cyclingrachelsmith.com and I'll send you my FREE 'Underspent Checklist'.

GET INVOLVED

Please feel free to like me, join me, stalk me, watch me, follow me and find out more about me on the following social media and communication channels:

- ▶ Website—www.cyclingrachelsmith.com
- ▶ Twitter—@CyclingRSmith
- ▶ LinkedIn—http://au.linkedin.com/pub/rachel-smith/32/349/b68
- ▶ Facebook—search for Rachel Smith (CyclingRachel Smith)

JOIN MY 14-WEEK PROGRAM

It took me 13 weeks to break my impulse shopping addiction and habit of buying 'stuff'.

I lead 14-week transformation programs with men and women who want to break their shopping addiction and buying habits. Join my Underspent program and I'll work with you, with a range of experts, advisors and mentors, and together we'll implement the seven steps in this book and celebrate your successes.

I'm committed. I want you to succeed and to accomplish change in your life, just as much as you do. What you will get includes:

- ▶ daily email
- ▶ personal accountability buddy
- ▶ weekly motivational videos and webinars
- ▶ seminars with mentors and specialist advisers
- ▶ worksheets and checklists
- ▶ question-and-answer Skype calls with me
- ▶ a private Facebook group.

Join me as we break old habits and save money! For more information please see www.cyclingrachelsmith.com or email me at Rachel@cyclingrachelsmith.com.

REFERENCES

The following sources are acknowledged. These people and publications were used for quotes, statistics, information, research and general reading.

1 Million Women, 1million-women.com.au

ABC News

Australian Bureau of Statistics Census data, March 2009, ABS, Canberra

Australian Bureau of Statistics 1997, *How Australians use their time, 1997*, cat. no. 4153.0, ABS, Canberra

Australian Churches Gambling Taskforce

Australian Council of Social Service (ACOSS)

Australian Government 2011, *Creating places for people: an urban design protocol for Australian cities*

BBC News

Becker, Joshua, becomingminimalist.com

Becker, Joshua 2010, *Simplify: seven guiding principles to help anyone declutter their home and life*

Benson, Dr April 2008, *To buy or not to buy: why we overshop and how to stop*, Trumpeter Books, Boston

Bianchi, Constanza & Birtwistle, Grete 2010, 'Sell, give away, or donate: an exploratory study of fashion clothing disposal behaviour in two countries', *The International Review of Retail, Distribution and Consumer Research*, vol. 20, no. 3, pp. 353–368

The Black Dog Institute

BMW Guggenheim Lab

Boston College

Botsman, Rachel

brisbanetimes.com.au

Byrne, Rhonda 2010, *The Secret*, Atria Books/Beyond Words, Hillsboro, Oregon

CNN Money, money.cnn.com

Commonwealth Bank of
   Australia

The Courier-Mail

de la Peña, Emily

Distractify.com

The Economist magazine

Ehrlich, Paul 1968, 1971, *The
   population bomb*, Buccaneer
   Books Inc, Cutchogue, New
   York (as well as other writings)

Farran, Lama at MaxWorth

Federal Reserve Board, *Survey of
   consumer finances*, USA

Goodman, Ellen

The Guardian newspaper

H2 Gambling Capital

Hamer, Edda

Hari, Johann 2015, *Chasing the
   scream: the first and last days of
   the war on drugs*, Bloomsbury
   Circus, London

House, Michelle, michellehouse.
   com.au

The Huffington Post

Independent Age,
   independentage.org

Kiosses, Stelios, psychotherapist

Lukas, Paul, *Fortune* magazine

McCrindle Research

The Money Charity,
   themoneycharity.org.uk

Mousina, Diana, Commonwealth
   bank economist

News.com.au, Cost of Living
   survey

Nolen-Hoeksema, Dr Susan

Roes, Debbie, Recovering
   Shopaholic blog,
   recoveringshopaholic.com

The share conference, www.
   peers.org

Statistic Brain

TEDxKurilpa

TuShare, www.tushare.com

UK Citizens Advice Bureau

Washington State University,
   www.wsu.edu

Wheel of Life, https://www.
   mindtools.com/pages/article/
   newHTE_93.htm

Wilson, Sarah

Zukin, Sharon 2005, *Point of
   purchase: how shopping changed
   American culture*, Routledge,
   Abingdon, Oxfordshire